Finding Grace in Lent

Journeying the Stations of the Cross

Greg Hildenbrand

April 4, 2015

John -

May your Lenten walk lead you to a more glorious resurrection experience of Easter!

Blessings,

Greg

Copyright © 2015 Hildenbrand

All rights reserved.

ISBN: 1505888719
ISBN-13: 978-1505888713

All rights reserved. Except as permitted under the U.S. Copyright Act of 1976, no part of this publication may be reproduced, distributed, or transmitted in any form or by any means, or stored in a database or retrieval system without prior written permission of the author.

Cover design by Billy Pilgrim (www.BillyPilgrim.biz)

Additional information and resources are available at
www.ContemplatingGrace.Com

Also by Greg Hildenbrand

Finding Grace in an Imperfect World

More information at

Dedication

I dedicate this book to the seeker of truth: the one who explores the depths of his or her being in search of a place of peace, that place of knowing, that place of sufficiency where God resides. I pray we will meet there one day.

Contents

Introduction

The story of the journey to Easter is a gruesome tale. We like to think of Easter eggs, chocolate bunnies, new clothes, and daffodils when we think of Easter. We cannot fully experience the joy and rebirth of the resurrection, however, without first traveling the road that takes us there. It is easy to think, "Oh, that is a sad story, and I am sorry Jesus had to go through that experience, but it was so long ago when people were such heathens. Praise God those days are over!" Unfortunately, if we want to know the resurrection in all its power and glory, we must first walk through the crucifixion in all its pain and humiliation.

Many of us wonder why Jesus had to die in such a brutal manner, and we wonder how his suffering and our salvation are related. Some theologians point out that sin cannot abide in the presence of God, sin being that which separates us from God. The price of sin is death; which in the days of Jesus was paid by having an animal killed on behalf of the sinner. Jesus, a sinless being, was punished for the sins of all of us, so the punishment was severe, indeed. Because of this sacrifice, however, God sees and judges us through Jesus – our sin is *filtered* out through the lens of Jesus. Without a sinless intermediary, our sin prevents us from being in the presence of God.

Not everyone is comfortable with the traditional explanations for the necessity of the suffering of Jesus. *Finding Grace in Lent* is especially for those who are uncertain because it does not try to justify the crucifixion. Rather, this book attempts to recreate the road to the cross and invites the reader to journey along it *with* Jesus. The premise is that the journey will provide its own justification for its end.

Embarking on a journey toward one's death is not easy, especially when one knows beforehand that the path will be excruciatingly painful. Ultimately, Lent is a journey to the resurrection. Jesus crosses the threshold from life to death to life and invites us to join him on this extraordinary voyage.

Finding Grace in Lent

The history of the *Stations of the Cross* begins with early attempts to recreate the holy places of Jesus' life in lands outside of Jerusalem. As Christianity spread throughout the world, it became increasingly difficult for many of the faithful to experience the important shrines in the Holy Land. The purpose of the Stations is to allow followers of Jesus to make a virtual, spiritual pilgrimage through the primary scenes of Christ's suffering and death. The traditional format for the Stations was formulated in the 17th century. Several of the 14 traditional stations, however, are not found in Scripture but in church tradition. In an effort to better align the Stations with Scripture, Pope John Paul II introduced a revised set of Stations in 1991, all of which are recorded in Scripture. Pope Benedict XVI formalized this revised set of the Stations in 2007, although the traditional stations are still found in many Catholic churches. *Finding Grace in Lent* follows the more recent, scriptural version of the Stations.

The *Stations of the Cross* hold a particular fascination and attraction for me, a non-Catholic. They provide the foundation for an intense experience of Lent. *Finding Grace in Lent* guides the reader along on a 47-day journey from Ash Wednesday to Easter. Two or 3 days are devoted to each of the Stations of the Cross, accompanied by a Scripture reading, a meditation, a spiritual discipline, and a prayer. The devotions for Sundays break from the Stations and are an opportunity to take a more expansive view of Lent. I have also included one of my songs for each Sunday, providing an alternative medium from which to experience Lent.

There is little that resembles grace during Lent. The resurrection we celebrate at Easter, however, is such a powerful and joyful conclusion that the road leading up to it is ultimately worthwhile. It is my prayer for you to find new insights on this deliberate journey to the cross.

Greg Hildenbrand
January 2015

Preparing for the Lenten Journey

Finding Grace in Lent is a workbook. I encourage you, the reader, to spend 15 or so minutes per day on each lesson. Find a quiet place with minimal distractions and focus your attention on each day's lesson. Although I have provided recommended spiritual disciplines and prayers, I encourage you to use whatever methods and techniques draw you closer to the cross. It is important, however, to do more than simply read what I have written. While reading the words of others can provide knowledge, it will not provide an *experience*. The purpose of meditating on the *Stations of the Cross* is to experience the scenes *with* Jesus, not to simply read about them. At the end of each lesson is space for you to write your thoughts and insights. Here is a brief overview of the spiritual disciplines recommended in this book:

Fasting

Fasting is a spiritual discipline that should make a person uncomfortable, but not miserable. It should be difficult, but not impossible to maintain. The point is to use the discomfort as a reminder of something important. Several different types of fasts are recommended throughout this study.

At its core, fasting is a break in routine. Generally, it involves some degree of sacrifice – intentionally giving up something of comfort, utility, or entertainment – in order to receive something else, like a spiritual insight. Too often, we cruise through a recurring rhythm in our days without stopping to contemplate meanings and significance. A fast, then, breaks that rhythm and shakes us out of our subconscious repetition and into a conscious awareness of the significance of the season. I have recommended several different types of fasts, each to last a few days before moving on to a different one. Feel free to design your own fasts, holding to the guideline that a fast should make you uncomfortable by breaking your routine.

Meditation

Meditation is a practice of actively focusing attention. Finding a quiet environment, absent of distraction is important. The purpose of the discipline of meditation is to focus one's attention on one thought or scene. Through this type of focused attention, we prepare ourselves to receive insights, inspiration, and wisdom related to the subject of our meditation.

Silence

Attaining silence is, perhaps, the most difficult of the spiritual disciplines to achieve. To experience a degree of silence, one must find a quiet environment away from televisions, computers, cell phones, and people. The goal is to free our minds of all distractions, including and especially our own internal dialogue. In silence, we listen. Often, we will hear nothing, and that is okay. The very experience of silence, however, lowers our heart rate and our blood pressure, while enhancing our ability to face whatever challenges confront us. The benefits of striving for and experiencing silence may not be immediately apparent. Once achieved, however, silence will bring us as close to experiencing God as we can come on the Earth.

Ash Wednesday

By the sweat of your face you shall eat bread until you return to the ground, for out of it you were taken; you are dust, and to dust you shall return.
Genesis 3:19

Meditation

The season of Lent begins with Ash Wednesday, a day of prayer and fasting. It is a day to remember that each of us – the greatest and the least, the rich and the poor, young and old, male and female, every race, every ethnic group, and every social class – is made from the stuff of the earth. Eventually, our bodies will return to the stuff of the earth. In that sense, we are equal, and that realization is cause for humility – before God and before humankind.

The traditional Ash Wednesday worship service closes with the imposition of ashes on the foreheads of attendees. The ash mixture contains olive oil mixed with the burned remains of the palms used during the previous year's Palm Sunday celebration. The palms-turned-to-ashes remind us that our joys and our sorrows belong together – they are two manifestations of the same experience. Where ashes normally represent death and sorrow, these ashes are the remains of a celebration. Contained within each of us is joy and sorrow, life and death.

Spiritual discipline

Attend an Ash Wednesday worship service. Have the ashes imposed on your forehead. When you arrive home, find a quiet place and dedicate 10 minutes to reflect on the significance of having this visible sign of torture and death imposed on you. Close your eyes. What do you see? What are you feeling? How will you walk with Jesus on this journey to the cross?

Prayer

Lord Jesus, as I begin this Lenten journey to the cross with you, remind me to approach this time with a humble heart and an open mind. Dust to dust, and ashes to ashes; I commit my life to your love and care. Amen.

Grace found

Station 1

Jesus in the Garden of Gethsemane

He came out and went, as was his custom, to the Mount of Olives; and the disciples followed him. When he reached the place, he said to them, "Pray that you may not come into the time of trial." Then he withdrew from them about a stone's throw, knelt down, and prayed, "Father, if you are willing, remove this cup from me; yet, not my will but yours be done." Then an angel from heaven appeared to him and gave him strength. In his anguish he prayed more earnestly, and his sweat became like great drops of blood falling down on the ground. When he got up from prayer, he came to the disciples and found them sleeping because of grief, and he said to them, "Why are you sleeping? Get up and pray that you may not come into the time of trial."

Luke 22:39-46

Thursday after Ash Wednesday

Station 1, Day 1: Jesus in the Garden of Gethsemane

He came out and went, as was his custom, to the Mount of Olives; and the disciples followed him. When he reached the place, he said to them, "Pray that you may not come into the time of trial." Luke 22:39-40

Meditation

The first Station of the Cross is in the Garden of Gethsemane on the Mount of Olives. This scene occurs after the Last Supper, when Jesus identified Judas as the one who would betray him. After Judas runs out to the Temple authorities, Jesus takes three of his disciples to a quiet place in the Garden, in the dead night. He wanders a few steps away from them and utters his first prayer to those disciples, warning them to pray not to fall into a time of trial.

Today, over two thousand years later, Jesus prays for us that we may not come into the time of trial. Our trials test us. In our legal system, a trial is held to determine guilt or innocence and to determine the truth. At the trial's end, the person is judged to be innocent or guilty. While trials are an inevitable part of life, we do not want to face a heavenly trial without being found innocent through the blood and saving grace of Jesus.

Spiritual discipline

Fast for the next 4 days by waking up and starting your day 15 minutes earlier than usual, using the time for study, reflection, and prayer. When you wake up and realize it is early, remember Jesus praying in the Garden. Whenever you feel tired throughout the day, remember Jesus asking for "this cup" to be removed from him. As you prepare for bed in the evening, feeling a little more tired than usual, remember Jesus' sweat falling like great drops of blood onto the ground.

Prayer

Loving Lord, we know we cannot avoid all of the trials of life, but we can know you will use our trials for good. Walk with us through our time of trial, even as we walk with you to the cross. In your holy name we pray. Amen.

Grace found

Friday after Ash Wednesday

Station 1, Day 2: Jesus in the Garden of Gethsemane

Then he withdrew from them about a stone's throw, knelt down, and prayed, "Father, if you are willing, remove this cup from me; yet, not my will but yours be done." Then an angel from heaven appeared to him and gave him strength. In his anguish he prayed more earnestly, and his sweat became like great drops of blood falling down on the ground. Luke 22:41-44

Meditation

Jesus goes off by himself to pray, a short distance from his disciples. In agony, he sweats profusely, knowing what is about to come. The pain and the humiliation he is about to endure has already been revealed to him. He begins his prayer with a request for mercy, pleading, "Father, if you are willing, remove this cup from me." Even God incarnate in Jesus did not wish to enter this trial unless it was necessary. He concludes his prayer with submission, stating, "Yet, not my will but yours be done." Remarkably, once he submits, an angel from heaven gives him strength.

Sometimes we put off doing that which we know must be done. Jesus came to earth to allow us to experience God, and for God to experience the worst the Earth has to offer. Only by suffering in the way Jesus did in his final hours can we know that God effectively empathizes with us during our worst hours of suffering. God has been there through the sacrifice of Jesus.

Spiritual discipline

Meditate for 10 minutes on a current trial or challenge you are facing. Perhaps an illness, a troubled relationship, or a difficult decision that is pending and weighing heavily upon you. How are you being judged in this trial? As you experience it, what are you learning about yourself? How will this trial strengthen you? Are you afraid? Will it cause pain? How might this fit within God's will?

Prayer

God of power and might, give me strength in my time of trial. Help me understand how to submit to your will and to faithfully do what you call me to do. Remind me of your presence, every step of the way. Remind me that you have walked this way before. Amen.

Grace found

Saturday after Ash Wednesday

Station 1, Day 3: Jesus in the Garden of Gethsemane

When he got up from prayer, he came to the disciples and found them sleeping because of grief, and he said to them, "Why are you sleeping? Get up and pray that you may not come into the time of trial." Luke 22:45-46

Meditation

The disciples are seemingly unaware of Jesus' agitation. They are exhausted and confused from the events at the Last Supper, and they are weary from the lateness of the night. Between being emotionally drained and physically tired, they fall asleep. Jesus wakes them up and tells them to pray not to come into the "time of trial."

Can we actually avoid this "time of trial?" I suspect we cannot. Rather, I believe Jesus is warning us to prepare for our times of trial. As we walk with Jesus along this sorrowful road to Golgotha, we are reminded that we must sometimes travel through the valley of the shadow of death in order to arrive at the new life on the other side.

Spiritual discipline

Find a quiet place and enter a time of silence for 10 minutes. Attempt to let go of the trials of the moment – your to do list, your stressors at work or home, and the pressing needs of the family. Deliberately turn off your inner dialogue by acknowledging thoughts as they come to you, then letting them go. Breathe deeply and internalize whatever degree of silence you can attain. There is no pressure to receive insights or inspiration. Experiencing silence is sufficient.

Prayer

Strong and silent God, reveal yourself to me in my silence. Allow me to feel your presence and to let it strengthen and comfort me, secure in the knowledge that I do not walk this journey alone. Amen.

Grace found

First Sunday in Lent

Then he said to them, "I am deeply grieved, even to death; remain here, and stay awake with me." And going a little farther, he threw himself on the ground and prayed, "My Father, if it is possible, let this cup pass from me; yet not what I want but what you want." Then he came to the disciples and found them sleeping; and he said to Peter, "So, could you not stay awake with me one hour? Stay awake and pray that you may not come into the time of trial; the spirit indeed is willing, but the flesh is weak." Matthew 26:38-41

Meditation

The image of Jesus in the Garden of Gethsemane can be mistaken for one of peace. It is dark and quiet, and the disciples are sleeping. Jesus, however, is agitated and anxious. No amount of physical exhaustion will grant him sleep.

As we experience Jesus in the Garden, we are advised to take special care to stay awake with Jesus, rather than falling asleep with the disciples. This is the first Station of the Cross and the journey is beginning. Remain alert!

Spiritual discipline

Attend worship at the church of your choice. Hold the picture of Jesus, desperately praying in the Garden, in your mind. In the evening, review the lessons, your notes, and your experience of the journey since Ash Wednesday.

Prayer

Lord Jesus, help me to stay awake with you and to remain in your presence as we begin this path together. Allow me a sense of the weight of sin laid upon you, for a portion of that sin belongs to me. Help keep me humble and thankful. Amen.

Song

The song *Jesus I am Here* is an affirmation of our determination to be among the faithful who remain true to Jesus through the events leading to his death. Listen to the song, follow the words, and recommit to staying awake and alert with Jesus through Easter Sunday and beyond.

Grace found

Jesus, I am Here

Jesus, take me to the wilderness

Jesus, take me to the wilderness

Tempt me with earth's finest wares,

In barren deserts of despair;

Jesus, take me to the wilderness.

Walking by my Savior's side, nothing need I fear;

On the road to Calvary, Jesus, I am here;

Jesus, I am here.

Jesus, I will follow and obey

Jesus, I will follow and obey;

Though my sin leads to the cross,

You, alone, will pay the cost;

Jesus, I will follow and obey.

Walking by my Savior's side, nothing need I fear;

On the road to Calvary, Jesus, I am here;

Jesus, I am here.

I'll walk with you into Jerusalem

I'll walk with you into Jerusalem;

To the slaughter of the Lamb,

The Savior and the saved as one;

I'll walk with you into Jerusalem.

Walking by my Savior's side, nothing need I fear;

On the road to Calvary, Jesus, I am here;

Jesus, I am here.

© 2006 Hildenbrand

Listen to this song at www.ContemplatingGrace.Com

Station 2

Jesus is betrayed by Judas

While he was still speaking, suddenly a crowd came, and the one called Judas, one of the twelve, was leading them. He approached Jesus to kiss him; but Jesus said to him, "Judas, is it with a kiss that you are betraying the Son of Man?"
Luke 22:47-48

Monday after the First Sunday in Lent

Station 2, Day 1: Jesus is betrayed by Judas and arrested

While he was still speaking, suddenly a crowd came, and the one called Judas, one of the twelve, was leading them. He approached Jesus to kiss him… Luke 22:47

Meditation

The second Station of the Cross occurs with Jesus still in the Garden of Gethsemane. He returns to his disciples and finds them asleep. A crowd of soldiers and curious on-lookers arrive, led by Judas. The Temple authorities needed an insider, like Judas, in order to capture Jesus for perhaps two reasons. First, they needed someone who was aware of Jesus' movements so they could capture him when he was away from the crowds. Second, they needed someone who knew Jesus well enough to recognize him in the dark.

The agreed upon signal, from Judas to the guards, was a kiss. Judas would go to Jesus, kiss him, and the guards would grab Jesus and take him back to the High Priest. It is ironic that Judas chooses a sign of affection to commit this act of deceit and betrayal.

Spiritual Discipline

Fast for the next 3 days by altering what you eat for lunch. Perhaps eat only an apple, or at least a significantly smaller quantity of food than normal. When you finish lunch and do not feel satiated, remember the kiss of Judas in the Garden. When hunger pangs return in the afternoon, remember Jesus being betrayed by a friend. When you are so hungry you feel you can barely wait until suppertime, imagine the stunned surprise of Jesus being betrayed with a symbol of affection.

Prayer

Loving Lord Jesus, I remember your betrayal on your last night on earth. I remember not only that you were betrayed, but that you were betrayed with an act of love. The pain of betrayal is deep, but the pain of betrayal by a loving act must be deeper still. Teach me to love you and others without a trace of betrayal. Amen.

Grace found

Tuesday after the First Sunday in Lent

Station 2, Day 2: Jesus is betrayed by Judas and arrested

...but Jesus said to him, "Judas, is it with a kiss that you are betraying the Son of Man? Luke 22:48

Meditation

The scene of the second Station of the Cross ends with a question: *Judas, do you betray me with a kiss?* When we consider the fateful evening to this point – from the emotional Last Supper, to praying in such agony as to have sweat falling like drops of blood – we can imagine the incredulity Jesus experienced at being approached by a betraying friend with a kiss.

What about us? Do we speak and act as if we love and are devoted to Jesus in one moment, and then turn around and speak and act as if we do not know who Jesus is? Are we not doing the same thing as Judas – betraying our Savior with a kiss?

Spiritual Discipline

Meditate for 10 minutes, focusing on what it means to love and follow Jesus. Consider the ways you betray Jesus. Consider the situations in which you are most likely to do so. Be careful not to become overwhelmed with guilt, for Jesus has already forgiven this shortcoming in us. Even so, it is important that we examine our own betrayals of Jesus and others.

Prayer

Loving and understanding Lord, please forgive me for my acts of betrayal of you. While it is not my intent to make you relive your suffering in the Garden, I fear that is what occurs. Your love is ever-patient and enduring, and for that I am unspeakably grateful. Amen.

Grace found

Wednesday after the First Sunday in Lent

Station 2, Day 3: Jesus is betrayed by Judas and arrested

While he was still speaking, suddenly a crowd came, and the one called Judas, one of the twelve, was leading them. He approached Jesus to kiss him; but Jesus said to him, "Judas, is it with a kiss that you are betraying the Son of Man?
Luke 22:47-48

Meditation

We might consider the method of Judas' betrayal as *passive-aggressive.* Passive-aggressive behavior expresses hostility in indirect ways, such as by sarcastic criticisms that are lightly covered to make them sound like a compliment. This type of behavior is particularly infuriating because it is doubly dishonest and, as such, doubly hurtful. When someone is angry with us, or when someone otherwise wishes to hurt us, it is one thing for them to speak their anger in direct and hurtful ways. When someone attempts to hurt us in *indirect* ways, however, such as betraying us with a kiss, we are left with confusion added to the hurt.

That Judas betrayed Jesus to the authorities is one thing – the initiating act in the series of events leading to the crucifixion. That Judas betrayed Jesus by approaching him as a loving brother must have added disappointment to the hurt.

Spiritual Discipline

Find a quiet place and enter a time of silence for 10 minutes. Attempt to let go of the trials of the moment – your to do list, your stressors at work or home, the pressing needs of family. Deliberately turn off your inner dialogue by acknowledging thoughts as they come to you, then letting them go. Breathe deeply and internalize whatever degree of silence you can attain. There is no pressure to receive insights or inspiration. Experiencing silence is sufficient.

Prayer

Patient and understanding Lord, as I strive to comprehend the nature in which you were betrayed, help me better grasp the passive-aggressive manner in which I may hurt others. Help me to be honest and direct as I interact with you and with others, always speaking the truth, with love and respect. Amen.

Station 3

Jesus is condemned by the Sanhedrin

When day came, the assembly of the elders of the people, both chief priests and scribes, gathered together, and they brought him to their council. They said, "If you are the Messiah, tell us." He replied, "If I tell you, you will not believe; and if I question you, you will not answer. But from now on the Son of Man will be seated at the right hand of the power of God." All of them asked, "Are you, then, the Son of God?" He said to them, "You say that I am." Then they said, "What further testimony do we need? We have heard it ourselves from his own lips."

Luke 22:66-71

Thursday after the First Sunday in Lent

Station 3, Day 1: Jesus is condemned by the Sanhedrin

When day came, the assembly of the elders of the people, both chief priests and scribes, gathered together, and they brought him to their council. They said, "If you are the Messiah, tell us." Luke 22:66-67a

Meditation

The third station of the cross occurs at daybreak on the Friday morning after the Last Supper. Jesus, having likely been awake all night, is taken to an assembly of the Sanhedrin, the group of religious leaders. This is the first formal trial of Jesus. The Temple authorities attempt to entice him to commit *blasphemy*, to admit being the Son of God. Unlike Judas, the Sanhedrin challenge Jesus directly. They immediately ask if he is the Messiah, the chosen one of God.

Jesus had spent the previous several years preaching and performing miracles in public places for all to hear and see. There was no doubt he possessed uncanny insights and powers, the likes of which none in the Temple could match. Jesus was a threat to the Temple leaders and their way of life, and this council was determined to find him guilty of some offense that would give them reason to have him killed.

Spiritual Discipline

Fast for the next 4 days by staying awake 15 minutes longer than usual. Utilize the extra time for meditation, study, and journaling. As you struggle to stay awake, remember Jesus being demeaned before the religious court. As you feel more tired than usual the next day, remember Jesus on trial before those who understood God far less than he did.

Prayer

Patient Lord, you have been put on trial and found to be worthy of my praise and thanksgiving. Remind me not to put you on trial again. Give me the strength not to waiver in my belief in your divine nature and your constant presence with me. Amen.

Grace found

Friday after the First Sunday in Lent

Station 3, Day 2: Jesus is condemned by the Sanhedrin

He replied, "If I tell you, you will not believe; and if I question you, you will not answer. But from now on the Son of Man will be seated at the right hand of the power of God." Luke 22:67b-69

Meditation

Because Jesus had been very public in his ministry, and because he had not tried to hide his oneness with God, he was defiant in his response to the Temple council questioning. When they asked if he was the Messiah, he told them they would not believe him, even if he told them! This is the pinnacle of unbelief – that when the truth stands before us, as Jesus stood before the Sanhedrin, we still do not believe.

Jesus had embarrassed the Temple authorities in the past by answering their public questioning in ways that illustrated how much greater his knowledge of God was than theirs. He points out their hypocrisy by noting that they would not be willing to answer Jesus' questioning of them.

Spiritual Discipline

Meditate for 10 minutes about your faith. Why do you believe in Jesus? If you do not have faith in Jesus, or if your faith waivers, what would it take to strengthen your faith? Picture Jesus on trial before the religious authorities of the day. What if Jesus was called before your church today – would he be found guilty of religious crimes?

Prayer

Enduring Lord, strengthen my faith in you. Help me to more fully understand who you were and who you are to me today. Let my faith establish a connection to you that cannot be broken by the ebb and flow of my days. Amen.

Grace found

Saturday after the First Sunday in Lent

Station 3, Day 3: Jesus is condemned by the Sanhedrin

All of them asked, "Are you, then, the Son of God?" He said to them, "You say that I am." Then they said, "What further testimony do we need? We have heard it ourselves from his own lips." Luke 22:70-71

Meditation

At first glance, Jesus' response does not seem to be the admission the Sanhedrin concludes it to be. They ask if he is the Son of God, and he responds, "You say that I am." The phrase that likely sets his accusers off is "I am," which is the name of God recorded in the book of Exodus, as given to Moses at the burning bush.

Once Jesus' words provide the court the proof they are looking for – that he is claiming to be the Son of God – they send Jesus off to the Roman authorities who govern that particular region. The Sanhedrin are allowed to provide religious services to the people, but are not allowed to crucify those they believe to be worthy of crucifixion.

Spiritual Discipline

Enter a time of silence for 10 minutes. Attempt to let go of the trials of the moment – your to do list, your stressors at work or home, the pressing needs of family. Deliberately turn off your inner dialogue by acknowledging thoughts as they come to you, then letting them go. Breathe deeply and internalize whatever degree of silence you can attain. There is no pressure to receive insights or inspiration. Experiencing silence is sufficient.

Prayer

Jesus, the Christ, the Son of Man and Son of God, you are my salvation. My ancestors accused you of being exactly who you are – the Son of God. Their reaction was to have you killed. May my reaction be to give you the praise and glory you deserve. Amen.

Grace found

Second Sunday in Lent

So the soldiers, their officer, and the Jewish police arrested Jesus and bound him. First they took him to Annas, who was the father-in-law of Caiaphas, the high priest that year. Caiaphas was the one who had advised the Jews that it was better to have one person die for the people. John 18:12-14

Meditation

The Gospel of John adds additional detail to the time in the Garden and the trial before the Sanhedrin the next morning. Jesus is arrested by the Temple police, bound, and taken to a couple of the priests for questioning: Caiaphas, the high priest, and Annas. Earlier, Caiaphas had stated that it was better to have one person, i.e., Jesus, die than to have the entire Jewish way of life threatened, tenuous as their existence was under Rome. No doubt, Caiaphas feared Roman retaliation against the Jews for the unrest Jesus created.

The fact that some of his followers referred to him as their King further enflamed Roman concern because non-Roman kings could not be tolerated.

Spiritual Discipline

Attend worship at the church of your choice. Hold the picture of Jesus in your mind, bound and standing before the priests. In the evening, review the lessons, your notes, and your Lenten experience of the journey of this past week.

Prayer

Jesus, my Lord, keep me awake and alert on this journey to the cross with you. Help me understand the significance of the events as they relate to my salvation. Ponder with me the irony of the Son of God on trial before the religious authorities of the day. These things I ask in your most holy name, Amen.

Song

The song *I Need to Know* is a plea for revelation. My faith is often challenged by my inability to see, hear, or touch Jesus today in the same way I see, hear, and touch my friends and family. Faith is strengthened through these challenges, however. In John 20:29b, Jesus says, "Blessed are those who have not seen and yet have come to believe." Even so, sometimes we, like Doubting Thomas, desire additional and tangible proof.

Grace found

I Need to Know

Speak to me, speak to me, I need to know you hear;
Speak to me, in my hour of need, speak to me,
So I know you are near.

Help me believe, help me believe, for my faith is weak;
Help me believe, lift this veil from me, help me believe
For my faith is weak.

Don't be far from here; I need to know you are near.

Show a sign, show me a sign, I need to know you are near;
Show a sign, that I'll recognize, show a sign
So I know you are near.

Don't be far from here; I need to know you are near.
I need to know you are near.
I need to know...

© 2010 Hildenbrand

Listen to this song at www.ContemplatingGrace.Com

Station 4

Jesus is denied by Peter

Then they seized him and led him away, bringing him into the high priest's house. But Peter was following at a distance. When they had kindled a fire in the middle of the courtyard and sat down together, Peter sat among them. Then a servant-girl, seeing him in the firelight, stared at him and said, "This man also was with him." But he denied it, saying, "Woman, I do not know him." A little later someone else, on seeing him, said, "You also are one of them." But Peter said, "Man, I am not!" Then about an hour later still another kept insisting, "Surely this man also was with him; for he is a Galilean." But Peter said, "Man, I do not know what you are talking about!" At that moment, while he was still speaking, the cock crowed. The Lord turned and looked at Peter. Then Peter remembered the word of the Lord, how he had said to him, "Before the cock crows today, you will deny me three times." And he went out and wept bitterly.
Luke 22:54-62

Monday after the Second Sunday in Lent

Station 4, Day 1: Jesus is denied by Peter

Then they seized him and led him away, bringing him into the high priest's house. But Peter was following at a distance. When they had kindled a fire in the middle of the courtyard and sat down together, Peter sat among them. Then a servant-girl, seeing him in the firelight, stared at him and said, "This man also was with him." But he denied it, saying, "Woman, I do not know him."
Luke 22:54-57

Meditation

The fourth Station of the Cross occurs after Jesus is taken from the Garden of Gethsemane to the house of the high priest under the cover of darkness. Peter, who was with Jesus in the Garden, follows at a distance. A servant-girl, who was probably among the crowd witnessing Judas' betrayal of Jesus, recognizes Peter and reveals that Peter had been with Jesus in the Garden. Peter denies knowing Jesus.

Peter's reaction, while not being what we would hope from ourselves, is understandable. He was tired and confused. His beloved leader had been captured, bound, and led away. The life Peter had given up everything for was beginning to crumble. Denying Jesus to protect himself in this situation should not surprise us, nor make us think less of Peter or his devotion to Jesus.

Spiritual Discipline

Fast for the next 3 days by substituting water for whatever beverage you most commonly drink during the day. When you desire a cup of coffee or cola, remember Jesus being denied by one of his closest and most beloved disciples. When you miss your caffeine energy boost, remember how Jesus was kept awake through this entire night.

Prayer

Forgiving Savior, I empathize with Peter's denial of you because I, too, deny knowing you. When I fear looking foolish, or when I am not with people of faith, or when I am doing something I feel will disappoint you, I pretend as if I do not belong to you. Strengthen me, O Lord, to defend and make you known, regardless of the situation. Amen.

Tuesday after the Second Sunday in Lent

Station 4, Day 2: Jesus is denied by Peter

A little later someone else, on seeing him, said, "You also are one of them." But Peter said, "Man, I am not!" Luke 22:58

Meditation

In Jesus' day, assigning guilt to a person required two witnesses. In other words, if two people testified to witnessing someone doing wrong, that person was proclaimed guilty. Another person, presumably also among the crowd in the Garden, recognizes Peter as having been with Jesus. Once again, Peter denies any association with Jesus.

All of us are prone to weakness, particularly in times of great stress. Certainly, Peter was under great stress on this night. His future was uncertain. Would he, too, be taken into custody and suffer the same fate as Jesus?

Spiritual Discipline

Meditate for 10 minutes on Peter in the court of the high priest's house. There are crowds of agitated people milling around. Jesus is in custody there. See the dark sky above and the glow of the firelight, casting long shadows around you. What do you see and feel in that courtyard? Will you be found guilty of associating with Christ? Do you deny Christ when you ignore the needs of others? When you gossip? When you laugh at demeaning jokes?

Prayer

Long-suffering Lord Jesus; like Peter, I am not always faithful to you. Too often, I deny my relationship to you in both direct and indirect ways. Please give me the strength of Peter to remain with you, to stand by your side, and to walk with you to the end. Amen.

Grace found

Wednesday after the Second Sunday in Lent

Station 4, Day 3: Jesus is denied by Peter

Then about an hour later still another kept insisting, "Surely this man also was with him; for he is a Galilean." But Peter said, "Man, I do not know what you are talking about!" At that moment, while he was still speaking, the cock crowed. The Lord turned and looked at Peter. Then Peter remembered the word of the Lord, how he had said to him, "Before the cock crows today, you will deny me three times." And he went out and wept bitterly. Luke 22:59-62

Meditation

During their dinner at the Last Supper, before retiring to the Garden of Gethsemane to pray, before the Temple guards came to take him away, Jesus reveals an amazing insight about Peter. Jesus tells his disciples about the events that will soon unfold and how many followers will fall away from and deny him. Peter insists he will never deny Jesus. Then, Jesus says, "I tell you, Peter, the cock will not crow this day, until you have denied three times that you know me." (Luke 22:33b)

In the courtyard of the high priest, Peter is accused three times of being a follower of Jesus. And three times he denies it. And with the third denial, the cock crows, exactly as Jesus predicted. Jesus knows our frailties and loves us deeply in spite of them.

Spiritual Discipline

Find a quiet place and enter a time of silence for 10 minutes. Attempt to let go of the trials of the moment – your to do list, your stressors at work or home, the pressing needs of family. Deliberately turn off your inner dialogue by acknowledging thoughts as they come to you, then letting them go. Breathe deeply and internalize whatever degree of silence you can attain. There is no pressure to receive insights or inspiration. Experiencing silence is sufficient.

Prayer

Patient and understanding Lord of my life, accept and forgive my human weaknesses. Allow me to feel your loving and accepting presence in times of joy, in times of despair, and in all times in between. Amen.

Grace found

Station 5

Jesus is judged by Pilate

Pilate then called together the chief priests, the leaders, and the people, and said to them, "You brought me this man as one who was perverting the people; and here I have examined him in your presence and have not found this man guilty of any of your charges against him. Neither has Herod, for he sent him back to us. Indeed, he has done nothing to deserve death. I will therefore have him flogged and release him." Then they all shouted out together, "Away with this fellow! Release Barabbas for us!" (This was a man who had been put in prison for an insurrection that had taken place in the city, and for murder.) Pilate, wanting to release Jesus, addressed them again; but they kept shouting, "Crucify, crucify him!" A third time he said to them, "Why, what evil has he done? I have found in him no ground for the sentence of death; I will therefore have him flogged and then release him." But they kept urgently demanding with loud shouts that he should be crucified; and their voices prevailed. So Pilate gave his verdict that their demand should be granted. He released the man they asked for, the one who had been put in prison for insurrection and murder, and he handed Jesus over as they wished. Luke 23:13-25

Thursday after the Second Sunday in Lent

Station 5, Day 1: Jesus is judged by Pilate

Pilate then called together the chief priests, the leaders, and the people, and said to them, "You brought me this man as one who was perverting the people; and here I have examined him in your presence and have not found this man guilty of any of your charges against him. Neither has Herod, for he sent him back to us. Indeed, he has done nothing to deserve death. I will therefore have him flogged and release him." Luke 23:13-17

Meditation

The fifth Station of the Cross occurs in the courtyard of Pilate, the Roman governor. The Temple authorities had found Jesus guilty of blasphemy and sentenced him to die. They did not, however, have the legal authority to crucify anyone, so they appeal to their Roman authority, Pilate. Rome, however, will not put someone to death for blasphemy, so the Temple leaders accuse Jesus of insurrection against the Roman government, saying he claimed to be King of the Jews. Pilate questions Jesus and finds him innocent, announcing he will have him flogged, and then release him.

In many ways, this situation is the third betrayal of Jesus in a matter of hours. First, Judas betrays Jesus in the Garden of Gethsemane. Second, Peter betrays Jesus in the courtyard of the chief priest. Finally, Jesus is betrayed by the Temple leaders, who alter the charge against him.

Spiritual Discipline

Fast for the next 4 days by waking up and starting your day 15 minutes earlier than usual, using the time for study, reflection, and prayer. When you wake up and realize it is early, remember Jesus before Pilate. Whenever you feel tired throughout the day, remember Jesus standing on trial after a sleepless night. As you prepare for bed in the evening, feeling more tired than usual, remember Jesus being accused by those he came to save.

Prayer

Jesus, my Lord and Savior, your suffering and torment is beyond my comprehension. Remind me, as I struggle through my days, that you have experienced suffering far worse than mine. Amen.

Friday after the Second Sunday in Lent

Station 5, Day 2: Jesus is judged by Pilate

Then they all shouted out together, "Away with this fellow! Release Barabbas for us!" (This was a man who had been put in prison for an insurrection that had taken place in the city, and for murder.) Pilate, wanting to release Jesus, addressed them again; but they kept shouting, "Crucify, crucify him!" A third time he said to them, "Why, what evil has he done? I have found in him no ground for the sentence of death; I will therefore have him flogged and then release him."

Luke 23:18-22

Meditation

The next scene at the fifth Station of the Cross is the crowd's reaction to Pilate as he pronounces Jesus not guilty. Pilate had a tradition of releasing a prisoner of the people's choice in honor of Passover. He believed this act helped to placate the people. The crowd not only shouts for the crucifixion of Jesus, but calls for the release of Barabbas, a convicted murderer and insurrectionist.

The humiliation of Jesus continues, for the crowd calling for his crucifixion likely contained many of the same people he taught and healed. His closest companions, the very people he dedicated his ministry to, are now calling for his death on a cross. Pilate, no friend to the Jews, again tries to release Jesus.

Spiritual Discipline

Meditate for 10 minutes on the betrayal of Jesus by the people. Picture yourself in the crowd. Hear the shouting and feel the emotion. Watch and listen as Pilate tries to convince the crowd of Jesus' innocence. What is Jesus doing? What are you doing?

Prayer

Lord Jesus, I confess I do not always know how best to love you, to follow you, and to show my devotion to you. Sometimes I find myself caught up in a crowd or some other distraction, and I find myself unintentionally denying you. In retrospect, I realize I, too, have betrayed you. Forgive me, Lord, and help me to keep my eyes fixed upon you. Amen.

Grace found

Saturday after the Second Sunday in Lent

Station 5, Day 3: Jesus is judged by Pilate

But they kept urgently demanding with loud shouts that he should be crucified; and their voices prevailed. So Pilate gave his verdict that their demand should be granted. He released the man they asked for, the one who had been put in prison for insurrection and murder, and he handed Jesus over as they wished.
Luke 23:23-25

Meditation

The crowd prevails, and Pilate condemns Jesus to death by crucifixion. The betrayal is complete, although Jesus' physical suffering has barely begun. Jesus has been tried and convicted by several human courts – the Sanhedrin, Pilate, and the crowds. He becomes a victim to what we, today, call *groupthink,* where a false idea is planted by a minority who repeat the idea until more people come to accept it as truth. Its truth, however, is accepted through repetition, instead of being established by fact.

Jesus' fate is decided. He will be killed in the most excruciating way known to man at the time, by being nailed to a cross and left to die.

Spiritual Discipline

Find a quiet place and enter a time of silence for 10 minutes. Attempt to let go of the trials of the moment – your to do list, your stressors at work or home, the pressing needs of family. Deliberately turn off your inner dialogue by acknowledging thoughts as they come to you, then letting them go. Breathe deeply and internalize whatever degree of silence you can attain. There is no pressure to receive insights or inspiration. Experiencing silence is sufficient.

Prayer

Innocent Lord, you were deserted by your followers of long ago. Give me the strength and insight not to desert you today. Amen.

Grace found

The Third Sunday in Lent

Pilate replied, "I am not a Jew, am I? Your own nation and the chief priests have handed you over to me. What have you done?" Jesus answered, "My kingdom is not from this world. If my kingdom were from this world, my followers would be fighting to keep me from being handed over to the Jews. But as it is, my kingdom is not from here." Pilate asked him, "So you are a king?" Jesus answered, "You say that I am a king. For this I was born, and for this I came into the world, to testify to the truth. Everyone who belongs to the truth listens to my voice." John 18:35-37

Meditation

The Gospel of John provides information about Pilate's questioning of Jesus that is not found in the other Gospels. Jesus makes clear that he has a kingdom, although not one of this world. Jesus is not referring to an earthly kingdom, and that causes considerable confusion. One of the reasons many people followed him is because they mistook him for an earthly king, one that would overthrow the oppressive Roman government. They were disillusioned when Jesus refused to use the powers he displayed throughout his ministry to save himself from his gruesome end.

Jesus tells Pilate that he came to testify to the truth. John 18:38 records Pilate as asking, "What is truth?" If Jesus answered the question, his response was not recorded.

Spiritual discipline

Attend worship at the church of your choice. Hold the picture of Jesus before Pilate in your mind. In the evening, review the lessons, notes, and experience of your Lenten journey of this past week.

Prayer

Jesus, my King, reveal your kingdom to me so I can reside there with you. Remind me to hold loosely to the kingdom of earth, for this will not be my home forever. I need to focus on you, your truth, and the kingdom of heaven, where you rule. Amen.

Song

The song *Take in Remembrance* is about the sacrament of communion, which Jesus established at the Last Supper. This ritual helps us internalize our relationship with Jesus by actually eating and drinking elements that represent his body and blood.

Take in Remembrance

Come, ye laden with heavy loads, I will give you rest,
At the table prepared for you, and by my Spirit blessed;
Receive the bread and wine, this body and blood are mine,
Spilled to cover the sins of time, and set my people free.
Oh, remember my broken body, broken on Calvary's tree,
When you take of it, take in remembrance of me.
When you take of it, take in remembrance of me.
Though my children may wander far,
I know each one by name;
And like a shepherd I seek them out,
And tend the lost and lame.
A covenant of grace, sealed on the cross: I took your place,
That sin no longer will separate, my people from their God.
Oh, remember the blood I poured out,
Poured out on Calvary's tree,
When you take of it, take in remembrance of me.
When you take of it, take in remembrance of me.
Receive the bread and wine, this body and blood are mine,
Spilled to cover the sins of time, and set my people free.
Oh, remember my broken body, broken on Calvary's tree,
When you take of it, take in remembrance of me.
When you take of it, take in remembrance of me.

© 2002 Hildenbrand

Listen to this song at www.ContemplatingGrace.Com

Station 6

Jesus is scourged and crowned with thorns

Now the men who were holding Jesus began to mock him and beat him; they also blindfolded him and kept asking him, "Prophesy! Who is it that struck you?" They kept heaping many other insults on him. Luke 22:63-65

And the soldiers wove a crown of thorns and put it on his head, and they dressed him in a purple robe. They kept coming up to him, saying, "Hail, King of the Jews!" and striking him on the face. John 19:2-3

Monday after the Third Sunday in Lent

Station 6, Day 1: Jesus is scourged and crowned with thorns

Now the men who were holding Jesus began to mock him and beat him; they also blindfolded him and kept asking him, "Prophesy! Who is it that struck you?" They kept heaping many other insults on him. Luke 22:63-65

Meditation

Pilate hands Jesus over to the Roman soldiers to be mocked, beaten, and scourged. This was all a part of the pre-crucifixion humiliation intended to show what happens to those who dare to challenge the authority of Rome. Jesus is blindfolded and the guards begin the flogging, which consisted of whipping Jesus, probably on the back, with cords containing small stones and bones intended to not only leave bloody stripes on one's back, but also to rip off pieces of flesh and tissue. Tradition holds that Jesus received 39 lashes. Forty lashes was believed to be the number that would cause death.

This means that Jesus is flogged to a point of still being alive, but just barely. The soldiers hurl various insults at Jesus throughout the flogging process. We wonder if Jesus even heard any of the taunting through the pain.

Spiritual Discipline

Fast for the next 3 days by altering what you eat for lunch. Perhaps eat only an apple, or at least a significantly smaller quantity of food than normal. When you finish lunch and do not feel satiated, remember Jesus being flogged. When hunger pangs return in the afternoon, picture the stripes on Jesus' back. When you are so hungry you feel you can barely wait until suppertime, remember Jesus, beaten and broken, only able to stand because he is tied to a post.

Prayer

Lord Jesus, your suffering at the hands of your betrayers is unimaginable. Remind me during my instances of suffering, Lord, that you have been there. Let my suffering be part of my walk with you, an offering to you as a sign of my submission. Amen.

Grace found

Tuesday after the Third Sunday in Lent

Station 6, Day 2: Jesus is scourged and crowned with thorns

And the soldiers wove a crown of thorns and put it on his head, and they dressed him in a purple robe. John 19:2

Meditation

Upon completion of the flogging, Jesus is bloody, swollen, and probably beaten beyond recognition. His humiliation at the hands of the Romans is actually ratcheted up another notch by dressing him as a mock king. They make and place a crown of thorns on his head. If Jesus was capable of feeling more physical pain at this point, he would have cringed at the thorns being pressed into his skull. They put a purple robe – the color of royalty – over his shredded skin and paraded him around for the people to gaze upon their "King."

"Some King!" the people likely thought, as they gazed upon this barely living image of shredded human flesh. If he were truly the Son of God, and if he truly had the power to save others, why would he not save himself? Was he unable, or simply unwilling?

Spiritual Discipline

Meditate for 10 minutes on Jesus, with his purple robe and crown of thorns. Imagine yourself in the scene, with soldiers dragging Jesus around, mocking him before the crowds. What do you see? What do you hear? How does it make you feel to be a part of the crowd?

Prayer

Lord of unspeakable suffering, I am a witness to your unjust torture, and I weep for your pain. I walk beside you, today, as I remember your suffering. Amen.

Grace found

Wednesday after the Third Sunday in Lent

Station 6, Day 3: Jesus is scourged and crowned with thorns

They kept coming up to him, saying, "Hail, King of the Jews!" and striking him on the face. John 19:3

Meditation

Supporters of Jesus in the crowd – certainly there were some present – were in a serious dilemma. Because Jesus was being crucified for insurrection, any overt displays of support for him could be interpreted as their support for his alleged defiance of Roman authority. Perceived supporters might suffer the same fate. As the soldiers cried, "Hail, King of the Jews!" no one in the crowd dared to intervene. Even so, hearts who had loved him would be broken to see their Lord and friend in his current condition.

Jesus was probably completely dazed and incoherent at this point, falling from soldier to soldier as they tried to keep him upright for everyone to see. Weakened from the pain, blood loss, lack of sleep, and humiliation, Jesus was awash in a tidal wave of suffering, being pushed and shoved closer to the cross.

Spiritual Discipline

Find a quiet place and enter a time of silence for 10 minutes. Attempt to let go of the trials of the moment – your to do list, your stressors at work or home, the pressing needs of family. Deliberately turn off your inner dialogue by acknowledging thoughts as they come to you, then letting them go. Breathe deeply and internalize whatever degree of silence you can attain. There is no pressure to receive insights or inspiration. Experiencing silence is sufficient.

Prayer

Jesus, there are no words. The skin on my back crawls as I imagine the flogging. My head aches as I envision your crown of thorns. My body throbs as I try to imagine your pain. My heart aches as I picture this ultimate humiliation. There are no words, but I am present with you, nonetheless. Amen.

Grace found

Station 7

Jesus takes up his cross

After mocking him, they stripped him of the purple cloak and put his own clothes on him. Then they led him out to crucify him. Mark 15:20

Thursday after the Third Sunday in Lent

Station 7, Day 1: Jesus takes up his cross

After mocking him, they stripped him of the purple cloak and put his own clothes on him. Then they led him out to crucify him. Mark 15:20

Meditation

Jesus now begins his final earthly journey. He is required to carry his cross to Golgotha – the Hill of the Skull – where he will be crucified. Tradition implies this may have been a lengthy walk, from the Governor's courtyard to a hill outside the city walls. The road believed to be taken by Jesus is still there, marked as the *Via Dolorosa*, the Way of Suffering. Those traveling to the Holy Land can retrace the steps of Jesus, from his flogging to his death.

Scripture tells us that Jesus fell under the weight of his cross at least once. Church tradition indicates he fell many times.

Spiritual Discipline

Fast for the next 4 days by staying awake 15 minutes longer than usual. Utilize the extra time for study, reflection, prayer, and journaling. As you wait to retire, remember Jesus, stumbling under his cross. When you awake in the morning, sleepier than usual, remember the weight of the cross resting on Jesus' raw shoulders. When you yawn throughout the day, remember the Jesus walking the Via Dolorosa.

Prayer

Lord Jesus, my Savior and my King, I know you walked the road of suffering on my behalf. It is me, and not you, who is guilty of acting as if I am God. It is me, and not you, who is defiant against God's ultimate authority. It is me, and not you, who deserves to be punished. Forgive me, Lord. Amen.

Grace found

Friday after the Third Sunday in Lent

Station 7, Day 2: Jesus takes up his cross

After mocking him, they stripped him of the purple cloak and put his own clothes on him. Then they led him out to crucify him. Mark 15:20

Meditation

I have difficulty picturing whether Jesus continued on his way toward Golgotha because he really had no choice, or whether he was doing it consciously, knowing he had to finish the work he had begun. Jesus displayed a divine power he could call upon at will throughout his ministry, focusing the power of heaven onto earthly suffering. Certainly, he could have mustered the power to put an end to his horrendous suffering. One would believe he could have, with a word, turned the pain onto those who were so anxious to inflict it upon him. But he did not. He just kept walking, apparently in silence.

Spiritual Discipline

Meditate for 10 minutes on the Via Dolorosa. Imagine yourself with the crowd beside the path. Roman soldiers are present everywhere. The broken and bloodied body of Jesus is slowly approaching, bent and struggling under the weight of the cross. He is barely recognizable. What do you experience in this moment?

Prayer

Jesus, as you walk the Via Dolorosa, give me the strength to not turn away from you. While I cannot remove the cross from your shoulders, encourage me to grab my cross and walk beside you. At the end of this road is death, but beyond is glory. Help me keep my eyes focused on the better times ahead, even as I acknowledge the pain of the present. Amen.

Grace found

Saturday after the Third Sunday in Lent

Station 7, Day 3: Jesus takes up his cross

After mocking him, they stripped him of the purple cloak and put his own clothes on him. Then they led him out to crucify him. Mark 15:20

Meditation

Once the business of humiliating this mock Jewish King was complete, the more serious business of crucifixion commenced. Jesus was stripped of his royal purple cloak and was returned to his normal attire. He was now treated as a common criminal and was paraded through the streets of the city for all to see. There was no physical strength on display here; only a broken wisp of the man he once had been. Jesus apparently accepted his fate, gathering whatever strength remained for the journey through town and to Golgotha.

It was a bitter cup prepared for our Lord, but he drank it with every ounce of humility and determination he could muster.

Spiritual Discipline

Find a quiet place and enter a time of silence for 10 minutes. Attempt to let go of the trials of the moment – your to do list, your stressors at work or home, the pressing needs of family. Deliberately turn off your inner dialogue by acknowledging thoughts as they come to you, then letting them go. Breathe deeply and internalize whatever degree of silence you can attain. There is no pressure to receive insights or inspiration. Experiencing silence is sufficient.

Prayer

Suffering Lord Jesus, as you struggled to carry your cross to the Hill of the Skull, I pray the knowledge that your suffering was a necessary part of God's plan for my salvation comforted you. As I walk in your memory today, reveal to me the love and strength required of you to complete this selfless act of sacrifice. Amen.

Grace found

The Fourth Sunday in Lent

Then Pilate took Jesus and had him flogged. And the soldiers wove a crown of thorns and put it on his head, and they dressed him in a purple robe. They kept coming to him, saying, "Hail, King of the Jews!" and striking him on the face. When the chief priests and the police saw him, they shouted, "Crucify him! Crucify him!" Pilate said to them, "Take him yourselves and crucify him; I find no case against him." The Jews answered him, "We have a law, and according to that law he ought to die because he has claimed to be the Son of God."
John 19:1b-3, 6-7

Meditation

It is interesting that the religious authorities were more threatened by Jesus than the Roman government. To be sure, Jesus' words and actions often made the Temple leaders look foolish. Pilate wanted to free Jesus, finding no case against him, but the priests insisted he be crucified. Pilate even told them to crucify him themselves. The writer of Matthew, in chapter 27, verse 24, records of the moment, "So when Pilate saw that he could do nothing, but rather that a riot was beginning, he took some water and washed his hands before the crowd, saying, 'I am innocent of this man's blood.'"

Even the Roman governor, Pilate, who was not known for compassion, was uncomfortable sentencing Jesus. Pilate was also uncomfortable with his own reluctant part in the events, washing his hands and claiming to absolve himself of any responsibility for the death of Jesus.

Spiritual discipline

Attend worship at the church of your choice. Hold the picture of Jesus in your mind, bound and on display before the crowds. People are screaming for the release of Barabbas, a convicted criminal, and for the crucifixion of Jesus. In the evening, review the lessons, your notes, and your experience of the journey of this past week.

Prayer

Jesus, my Lord and Savior, the emotional pain of seeing your followers turn on you in Pilate's court must have been dreadful. I fear that, had I been alive at the time, I might have been in the crowd, too. Today, however, I stand with you as a faithful follower in the truth. Amen.

Song

The song *Love That Will Not Let Me Go* is a taken from the 17th chapter of John, which records Jesus' prayer in the Garden of Gethsemane. In that prayer, Jesus makes three petitions. The first is that the suffering he is about to go through will accomplish its purpose. The second is for the protection and salvation of his followers, who he knows will have a difficult struggle after he is gone. The third group Jesus prays for is us, today. He prays that we, two thousand years later, will know God through him. Although Jesus prays not to be forgotten, the purpose is not to satisfy his ego. Rather, Jesus knows his followers – including us today – would need to remember him during their own times of trial.

Grace found

Love That Will Not Let Me Go (John 17)

Glorify, O God, your Son, now my work on earth is done,
So that I may glorify you, in this hour I now go through.
I long for the love that will not let me go,
That only in your presence can be known,
A love not of the earth, but perfect love from being One with you,
Love that will not let me go.
Guard, O God, these who remain, here on earth from evil's reign,
Sanctify your truth in love, that they, too, be One with us.
And long for the love that will not let me go,
That only in your presence can be known,
A love not of the earth, but perfect love from being One with you,
Love that will not let me go, no matter what the cost,
Once they know their God, they'll not be lost,
The Spirit will bestow a perfect love from being One with you,
Love that will not let me go.
Draw, O God, our lost sheep home, build their faith on you alone,
I in you and they in me, One in love eternally.
To long for the love that will not let me go,
That only in your presence they can know,
A love not of the earth, but perfect love from being One with you,
Love that will not let me go, no matter what the cost,
Once they know their God, they'll not be lost,
The Spirit will bestow a perfect love from being One with you,
Love that will not let me go.

© 2000 Hildenbrand

Station 8

Jesus is helped by Simon to carry his cross

As they led him away, they seized a man, Simon of Cyrene, who was coming from the country, and they laid the cross on him, and made him carry it behind Jesus.
Luke 23:26

Monday after the Fourth Sunday in Lent

Station 8, Day 1: Jesus is helped by Simon to carry his cross

As they led him away, they seized a man, Simon of Cyrene, who was coming from the country, and they laid the cross on him, and made him carry it behind Jesus. Luke 23:26

Meditation

Jesus is struggling with his cross, apparently going too slowly for the Roman soldiers. They grab a man from the crowd, Simon of Cyrene, and order him to carry Jesus' cross. We are not told if Simon of Cyrene even knows who Jesus is. He may have joined the crowd in order to see what was going on.

Regardless, Simon is enlisted to help Jesus with his burden. Scripture is not clear whether Simon was forced by the soldiers to help Jesus.

Spiritual Discipline

Fast for the next 2 days by substituting water for whatever beverage you most commonly drink during the day. When you desire a cup of coffee or cola, remember Simon of Cyrene carrying Jesus' cross. When you miss your caffeine energy boost, remember Jesus stumbling along in pain before him.

Prayer

Weary Lord, when my burdens become too heavy, I long for someone to help me carry them, as Simon of Cyrene did for you with your cross. Thank you for always being nearby to share my burdens. Amen.

Grace found

Tuesday after the Fourth Sunday in Lent

Station 8, Day 2: Jesus is helped by Simon to carry his cross

As they led him away, they seized a man, Simon of Cyrene, who was coming from the country, and they laid the cross on him, and made him carry it behind Jesus. Luke 23:26

Meditation

We do not know whether Simon of Cyrene would have helped Jesus carry his cross willingly. However, in his hour of most desperate need, Jesus received assistance. He might have received help because of the impatience of the soldiers, or because the soldiers feared he would die of exhaustion before they could crucify him, or perhaps because people were crying out from the crowd to get him help. Regardless of the reason, our long-suffering Jesus was given relief.

We can argue that Jesus was only given the assistance to hurry the journey to Golgotha. Even so, I believe there may have been some comfort to have the burden of the cross lifted from his shoulders, if only for a short time.

Spiritual discipline

Meditate for 10 minutes beside the Via Dolorosa as Jesus is carrying his cross. A Roman guard calls you out of the crowd to carry the cross for him. Do you go willingly? Do you feel honored, or do you feel you are now a party to this terrible injustice? Imagine Jesus stumbling before you. Feel the weight of the cross. Smell the scent of the timber.

Prayer

Lord Jesus, I am thankful that in one of the low points of this journey, you received assistance. You so willingly carry my burdens for me. Remind me to provide respite to others with their heavy loads. Amen.

Grace found

Station 9

Jesus meets the women of Jerusalem

A great number of the people followed him, and among them were women who were beating their breasts and wailing for him. But Jesus turned to them and said, "Daughters of Jerusalem, do not weep for me, but weep for yourselves and for your children. For the days are surely coming when they will say, 'Blessed are the barren, and the wombs that never bore, and the breasts that never nursed.' Then they will begin to say to the mountains, 'Fall on us'; and to the hills, 'Cover us.' For if they do this when the wood is green, what will happen when it is dry?"

Luke 23:27-31

Wednesday after the Fourth Sunday in Lent

Station 9, Day 1: Jesus meets the women of Jerusalem

A great number of the people followed him, and among them were women who were beating their breasts and wailing for him. But Jesus turned to them and said, "Daughters of Jerusalem, do not weep for me, but weep for yourselves and for your children." Luke 23:27-28

Meditation

After Simon of Cyrene has taken Jesus' cross, the journey along the Way of Suffering continues. At the 9th Station of the Cross are women in the crowd who are mourning for Jesus. He musters the strength to turn to them to say that they should not weep for him but for themselves and their children. He implies there will be suffering to come for all, and there will be time and reason for weeping at that time.

It is hard to imagine that Jesus predicted suffering for others that would be worse than what he was enduring at the time. He could have known, however, that suffering would come to all. Because he was leaving his earthly life, he would no longer be available to assist, comfort, and teach them.

Spiritual discipline

Fast for the next 2 days by waking up and starting your day 15 minutes earlier than usual, using the time for study, reflection, and prayer. When you wake up and realize it is early, remember Jesus warning others of the suffering to come, even as he was suffering. Whenever you feel tired throughout the day, remember Jesus, caring for others. As you prepare for bed in the evening, feeling more tired than usual, remember Jesus, whispering his warning to the women of Jerusalem.

Prayer

Faithful Lord, only you could find the strength to counsel those around you, even as your body is racked with pain and exhaustion. Let your actions along this road be an inspiration to me to encourage others as I walk my road. Amen.

Grace found

Thursday after the Fourth Sunday in Lent

Station 9, Day 2: Jesus meets the women of Jerusalem

"For the days are surely coming when they will say, 'Blessed are the barren, and the wombs that never bore, and the breasts that never nursed.' Then they will begin to say to the mountains, 'Fall on us'; and to the hills, 'Cover us.' For if they do this when the wood is green, what will happen when it is dry?"
Luke 23:29-31

Meditation

Jesus tells the weeping women to mourn for themselves and not for him. He then implies that in the time of trial it will be better for those who never bore children. Does he mean we will witness the suffering of children such that we will wish we never had children at all? I think that is exactly what he is saying. Apparently, times will become so troubling we will ask for the mountain to fall on and bury us.

We can only speculate about the times to which Jesus refers. Perhaps he is referencing the end times described in the Revelation of John. Perhaps they are a reference to the tribulations the people of Israel will go through in the generations following Jesus' death.

Spiritual discipline

Meditate for 10 minutes on Jesus' interaction with the women of Jerusalem. Picture yourself following him down the road, weeping, when he turns and tells you to weep for yourself. What sorrows would make you wish you were barren? What calamities would make you wish for death by burial under a mountain? Do Jesus' words make you feel closer to or more distant from Jesus?

Prayer

All-knowing Lord Jesus, you predict miserable times ahead for those of us on the earth. Help me to strengthen my connection to you so I will be better able to lean on you through whatever trials lay before me. Amen.

Grace found

Station 10

Jesus is Crucified

When they came to the place that is called The Skull, they crucified Jesus there with the criminals, one on his right and one on his left. When the centurion saw what had taken place, he praised God and said, "Certainly this man was innocent." Luke 12:33, 47

Friday after the Fourth Sunday in Lent

Station 10, Day 1: Jesus is crucified

When they came to the place that is called The Skull, they crucified Jesus there with the criminals, one on his right and one on his left. Luke 12:33

Meditation

Jesus was crucified on the hill known as Golgotha, also called The Skull. It is outside the walls of the city, and it is where executions were performed. Upon arriving at this place, his feet and hands are nailed to the cross, and he is raised up to die. Death by crucifixion comes from asphyxiation, because one must have the strength to raise their body against the binds of their hands and feet in order to breathe. Jesus, in an already desperately weakened state, may not have survived long on the cross.

Would Jesus have felt relief to be on the cross at last, where he could eventually be done with this torture?

Spiritual discipline

Fast for the next 3 days by altering what you eat for lunch. Perhaps eat only an apple, or at least a significantly smaller quantity of food than normal. When you finish lunch and do not feel satiated, remember Jesus being nailed to the cross. When hunger pangs return in the afternoon, remember Jesus struggling to muster the strength required of each breath he takes. When you are so hungry you feel you can barely wait until suppertime, remember Jesus hanging on the cross on a barren hill amongst criminals.

Prayer

Enduring Lord, my Savior, you died the tortured death of a lowly criminal. You seemed to be determined to suffer through every bit of human cruelty and physical pain that could possibly be endured. Help me to better understand the magnitude of your sacrifice for me. Amen.

Grace found

Saturday after the Fourth Sunday in Lent

Station 10, Day 2: Jesus is crucified

When the centurion saw what had taken place, he praised God and said, "Certainly this man was innocent." Luke 23:47

Meditation

Guilt and innocence on earth are determined by human beings and may or may not have relevance in God's eyes. Jesus was judged to be guilty by the Temple authorities, the Roman authorities, and by the crowds. He made no attempt to proclaim his innocence. He made no attempt at a divine intervention to relieve himself of his suffering. He accepted his fate with a grace unknown to us.

At the foot of the cross is a Roman soldier, stationed to keep the peace until Jesus' passing. He witnesses Jesus as he dies and recognizes that Jesus, indeed, was innocent. Although Scripture does not reveal *how* the soldier knew of Jesus' innocence, we can assume he deduced the injustice by the way Jesus carried himself throughout his crucifixion. Clearly, Jesus was unlike others this soldier had crucified.

Spiritual discipline

Meditate for 10 minutes on Jesus hanging on the cross between the criminals. Picture yourself at the foot of the cross, hearing the conversation between Jesus and the criminals. Watch as the Roman guard begins to understand that Jesus truly is the Messiah. Contemplate the sights and sounds of the scene.

Prayer

Lord Jesus, even as you are racked with pain and near death, you continue to care for those around you. You continue your faith that God has a worthy purpose for your suffering. Strengthen me to have a faith more like yours. Amen.

Grace found

The Fifth Sunday in Lent

It was nine o'clock in the morning when they crucified him. The inscription of the charge against him read, "The King of the Jews." And with him they crucified two bandits, one on his right and one on his left. Those who passed by derided him, shaking their heads and saying, "Aha! You who would destroy the temple and build it in three days, save yourself, and come down from the cross!" In the same way the chief priests, along with the scribes, were also mocking him among themselves and saying, "He saved others; he cannot save himself. Let the Messiah, the King of Israel, come down from the cross now, so that we may see and believe."

Mark 15:25-32a

Meditation

The Romans had no law mandating the crucifixion of someone claiming to be the Son of God. The Jews had a law condemning someone to death for claiming to be the Son of God, but no legal means by which to crucify him. So, the Romans crucified Jesus for insurrection, even after being found innocent by the governor. Jesus was crucified to appease the crowds. The justification for the sentence was that Jesus claimed to be a king, and thus was a threat to Rome.

In spite of his 3 years of ministry and miracles, the crowds were looking for further proof of Jesus' divinity. They wanted to see him miraculously remove himself from this situation. In the absence of some spectacular turn of events, Jesus was deemed a fraud. The people felt they needed to see one more miracle before they could believe.

Spiritual discipline

Attend worship at the church of your choice. Hold the picture of Jesus, nailed to the cross, in your mind. In the evening, review the lessons, your notes, and your experience of the journey of this past week.

Prayer

Loving and healing Lord, the people of your time felt they needed to see another miracle before they could believe in you as their Messiah. I believe, even though I have not seen. I feel your presence in my life, and I am thankful for your sacrifice. Amen.

Song

The song *The Blood of the Lamb,* is taken from John's Gospel record of the crucifixion and death of Jesus. This story is told through the point of view of an observer. The song is from a musical based on the Gospel of John, *A Perfect Love,* that I wrote in 1999.

Grace found

The Blood of the Lamb

John 19:16-42

He carried his cross to the Place of the Skull
Where they drove spikes deep into his hands;
They hung him up high for the world to behold,
Though he hardly looked like the same man.
Beaten and bleeding and struggling to breathe,
He hung until mid-afternoon,
Under a sign that read, "Here hangs the King of the Jews."
Near to the end he cried out, "I am thirsty,"
And was given a sponge full of wine,
He said, "It is finished," then lowered his head,
He gave up his spirit and died.
They pierced his side with a spear and then watched
As the blood and the water poured free,
The blood of the lamb and the water of life were released.
We had him removed from the cross to prepare
His body for burial there.
We wrapped him in burial cloths with a hundred
Pounds of the aloes and myrrh;
We laid him inside a new tomb and then wondered,
Could this be the way it all ends?
Sealed in a tomb and forsaken by God to our hands.

© 2000 Hildenbrand

Listen to this song at www.ContemplatingGrace.Com

Station 11

Jesus promises his kingdom to the repentant thief

When they came to the place that is called The Skull, they crucified Jesus there with the criminals, one on his right and one on his left. Then Jesus said, "Father, forgive them; for they do not know what they are doing." And they cast lots to divide his clothing.

Luke 23:33-34

One of the criminals who were hanged there kept deriding him and saying, "Are you not the Messiah? Save yourself, and us!" But the other rebuked him, saying, "Do you not fear God, since you are under the same sentence of condemnation? And we indeed have been condemned justly, for we are getting what we deserve for our deeds, but this man has done nothing wrong." Then he said, "Jesus, remember me when you come into your kingdom." He replied, "Truly I tell you, today you will be with me in paradise."

Luke 23:39-43

Monday after the Fifth Sunday in Lent

Station 11, Day 1: Jesus promises his kingdom to the repentant thief

When they came to the place that is called The Skull, they crucified Jesus there with the criminals, one on his right and one on his left. Then Jesus said, "Father, forgive them; for they do not know what they are doing." And they cast lots to divide his clothing. Luke 23:33-34

Meditation

I imagine Golgotha, the Skull, as a barren hill – a place of death. I picture a rocky, tree-less wasteland, where those condemned to die hang on their crosses with no protection from the sun, wind, or elements. I suspect the place was chosen because it added its own unique element of misery to an otherwise excruciating and humiliating end. This is the conclusion of the journey down the Via Dolorosa – a miserable path to a dismal destination.

Here at Golgotha is where we join Jesus at the 11th Station of the Cross – beaten raw, bleeding, exhausted, beset with pain, and nailed to a cross between two criminals. Even so, he seeks forgiveness for his persecutors, who have no idea what they are doing.

Spiritual discipline

Fast for the next 2 days by staying awake 15 minutes longer than usual. Use the time for study, meditation, prayer, and journaling. As you wait to retire, remember Jesus nailed to this place of death. When you awake in the morning, sleepier than usual, picture Jesus among the criminals. When you yawn throughout the day, remember Jesus – hungry, thirsty, beaten, and broken.

Prayer

Jesus on the cross, after your long and painful journey you end up here, at this horrible place of death. Yet, we have learned from you that to gain new life the old must first die. Given the physical shape of your body, death must come as a blessing. Help me to understand the lessons of the cross. Amen.

Grace found

Tuesday after the fifth Sunday in Lent

Station 11, Day 2: Jesus promises his kingdom to the repentant thief

One of the criminals who were hanged there kept deriding him and saying, "Are you not the Messiah? Save yourself, and us!" But the other rebuked him, saying, "Do you not fear God, since you are under the same sentence of condemnation? And we indeed have been condemned justly, for we are getting what we deserve for our deeds, but this man has done nothing wrong." Then he said, "Jesus, remember me when you come into your kingdom." He replied, "Truly I tell you, today you will be with me in paradise." Luke 23:39-43

Meditation

One of the criminals hanging beside Jesus mocks him, saying if he is the Messiah he should save himself. The other criminal admonishes his colleague in crime by confessing that they are getting the punishment they deserve for their crimes, but affirms that Jesus has done nothing wrong. The second criminal then asks Jesus to remember him when he comes into his kingdom. Jesus assures him he will be remembered.

Clearly, the second criminal is repentant. He accepts his fate as one he deserves, even as he recognizes that Jesus has done nothing to earn such an end. Therein is the key to our salvation – that we confess and repent of our sin and seek forgiveness.

Spiritual discipline

Meditate for 10 minutes on this scene. Picture Jesus nailed to the cross, showing compassion for the repentant criminal. How do you feel about the unrepentant criminal? Hold the picture in your mind and pay attention to the sights and sounds.

Prayer

Forgiving Lord, you showed mercy and forgiveness to the repentant criminal, as well as for those who crucified you. I ask for the same mercy and forgiveness today, understanding these are gifts I have not earned, nor do I deserve. Amen.

Grace found

Station 12

Jesus entrusts Mary and John to each other

Meanwhile, standing near the cross of Jesus were his mother, and his mother's sister, Mary the wife of Clopas, and Mary Magdalene. When Jesus saw his mother and the disciple whom he loved standing beside her, he said to his mother, "Woman, here is your son." Then he said to the disciple, "Here is your mother." And from that hour the disciple took her into his own home.
John 19:25-27

Wednesday after the fifth Sunday in Lent

Station 12, Day 1: Jesus entrusts Mary and John to each other

Meanwhile, standing near the cross of Jesus were his mother, and his mother's sister, Mary the wife of Clopas, and Mary Magdalene. John 19:25b

Meditation

At the 12th Station of the Cross, standing at the foot of his cross, are Jesus' mother, his aunt, and his friend – all named Mary. No doubt, they are overwhelmed with sorrow and a sense of utter powerlessness. Particularly in Jesus' day, women had little social standing anyway, but on this particular day they must have felt invisible. They had followed Jesus along the Via Dolorosa to Golgotha. They had witnessed the flogging, the mocking, and the tortured steps along the way with the cross.

Perhaps Jesus felt some relief knowing that not everyone who loved him had deserted him in his final hours. At least these three women remained with him to the end.

Spiritual discipline

Fast for the next 2 days by substituting water for whatever beverage you most commonly drink during the day. When you desire a cup of coffee or cola, remember Jesus, arranging for the care of his mother. When you miss your caffeine energy boost, remember Jesus, sleepless and thirsty on the cross.

Prayer

Jesus, my Savior, I pray you received some comfort in seeing your mother, aunt, and friend at the foot of your cross. I pray you receive some comfort today, as I kneel with them at the foot of your cross, a witness to the power manifested in your death. Amen.

Grace found

Thursday after the fifth Sunday in Lent

Station 12, Day 2: Jesus entrusts Mary and John to each other

When Jesus saw his mother and the disciple whom he loved standing beside her, he said to his mother, "Woman, here is your son." Then he said to the disciple, "Here is your mother." And from that hour the disciple took her into his own home. John 19:26-27

Meditation

The three women were not the only ones to remain with Jesus to the end. The disciple whom he loved, presumably John, was there, too. As Jesus looked down upon them, he was concerned for the care of his mother. In that day, a woman with no husband or sons to care for her was homeless and destitute. Although Scripture tells us that Mary had other sons, Jesus pledges his mother into John's care, and John into the care of his mother.

Sorrow is a heavy burden to bear alone. Jesus made sure John and Mary would have each other to share the load.

Spiritual discipline

Meditate for 10 minutes on this scene. Picture the three women and John at Jesus' feet, watching him struggle for each breath, wondering which breath will be his last. Imagine yourself with them at the foot of the cross. What do you see, hear, and feel? Who is in your life to share your burdens?

Prayer

Compassionate Lord, you cared for those you loved as long as you were able. Instead of wallowing in self-pity and despair, you looked after your loved ones, forgave your persecutors, and reassured a criminal of his salvation. Help me to learn from your example of serving others with every breath I am given. Amen.

Grace found

Station 13

Jesus dies on the cross

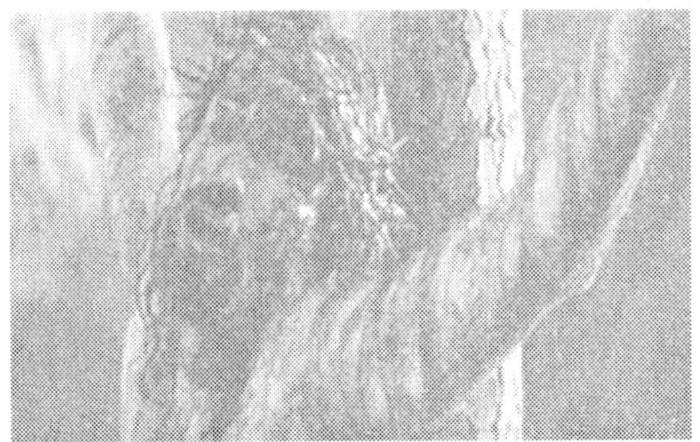

It was now about noon, and darkness came over the whole land until three in the afternoon, while the sun's light failed; and the curtain of the temple was torn in two. Then Jesus, crying with a loud voice, said, "Father, into your hands I commend my spirit." Having said this, he breathed his last.
Luke 23:44-45

Friday after the fifth Sunday in Lent

Station 13, Day 1: Jesus dies on the cross

It was now about noon, and darkness came over the whole land until three in the afternoon, while the sun's light failed; and the curtain of the temple was torn in two. Luke 23:44-45

Meditation

The symbolism of the torn curtain in the Temple at the 13th Station of the Cross is significant. This heavy curtain separated the area containing the Holy of Holies, which was where God was believed to reside. The area behind the curtain was only accessed on one day per year – the Day of Atonement – and then only by the High Priest. The curtain separated humanity from divinity, so when the curtain was torn at Jesus' death, access to God was granted to all. A heavy curtain separating this life from the next was torn, so there would be separation no more.

Jesus came to earth to make God known to us. When Jesus died and the curtain was torn, we not only had the example of God in Jesus, but actual *access* to God, who previously could only be accessed through the High Priest.

Spiritual discipline

Fast for the next 3 days by waking up and starting your day 15 minutes earlier than usual, using the time for study, reflection, and prayer. When you wake up and realize it is early, remember the curtain being torn in the Temple as Jesus breathed his last breath. Whenever you feel tired throughout the day, remember Jesus, giving up his spirit to God. As you prepare for bed in the evening, feeling more tired than usual, remember the direct access you now have to God, and be thankful.

Prayer

Almighty Lord, through the example of your life, I know more about God and what God expects of me. Through your death, I have access to you and God through prayer and meditation. Nothing can restrict that access, and for that, I am thankful. Amen.

Grace found

Saturday after the fifth Sunday in Lent

Station 13, Day 2: Jesus dies on the cross

Then Jesus, crying with a loud voice, said, "Father, into your hands I commend my spirit." Having said this, he breathed his last. Luke 23:46

Meditation

The last words Jesus utters as a living being on earth are to God, offering his spirit to God. It is a fitting end to a journey none of us would embark upon willingly. In the same way he began his ministry, as an act of obedience to God, he ended his ministry by turning the only thing he had left – his spirit – back to God. There is no hint of ego or legacy-seeking or bitterness. Jesus' entire life belonged to God, and when his life ended, he returned it to God. By earthly standards, these would not be "last words" worthy of posterity. Yet, they have endured for thousands of years as an uncommon expression of humility and submission.

After commending his spirit to God, his father, Jesus dies on the cross. The long, painful march to his physical death is complete, roughly18 or so hours after it began. In a typical crucifixion, the legs of the criminals are broken in the late afternoon to hasten death. A person on a cross whose legs are broken can no longer push themselves up in order to take a breath. Jesus dies before the leg-breaking is necessary, however, consistent with an Old Testament prophesy that none of his bones would be broken.

Spiritual discipline

Meditate for 10 minutes on this scene at Golgotha. Place yourself at the foot of the cross, looking up at Jesus as his breathing becomes more labored and less frequent. Hear the words, probably in a hoarse and breathless whisper, "Father, into your hands I commend my spirit." Experience the silence that follows.

Prayer

Crucified Lord, your long and painful journey has ended. I have walked with you from the Garden of Gethsemane to the hill of Golgotha. I have seen you tried and beaten, flogged and humiliated. What a sorrowful journey it has been. Amen.

Grace found

Palm Sunday

As he rode along, people kept spreading their cloaks on the road. As he was now approaching the path down from the Mount of Olives, the whole multitude of the disciples began to praise God joyfully with a loud voice for all the deeds of power that they had seen, saying, "Blessed is the king who comes in the name of the Lord! Peace in heaven, and glory in the highest heaven!"
Luke 19:36-38

Meditation

We now leave the Stations of the Cross for a day in order to celebrate Palm Sunday, which predates the first Station by several days. Palm Sunday is the beginning of the end for Jesus, who had intentionally avoided spending significant time in Jerusalem until now, knowing his appearance there would hasten his end. Yet, he could not avoid going to Jerusalem forever because that was the only place where his ministry could be successfully completed. Jerusalem was spiritual center and heart of the Jewish faith.

So, Jesus enters the city on a colt to parade-like celebrations. Jesus comes into his kingdom with power and glory. Unfortunately, the people misjudge the type of power he brought. They assumed he would overthrow the Roman government and set them free of its oppressive rule. Jesus, however, was bringing a different kind of kingdom and a different kind of freedom – spiritual, rather than physical freedom. Many in the crowds would not understand the difference and would soon feel deceived.

Spiritual discipline

Meditate for 10 minutes on Jesus' entry into Jerusalem, in the context of your recent journey through the Stations of the Cross. Knowing the journey Jesus is about to begin, what insights do you gain from this triumphal entry? How is it that he was treated like a king as he enters, and then crucified like a criminal a few days later?

Prayer

Jesus, you are my Lord of Lords and the King of my life. I celebrate your entry into Jerusalem, not for the pain to come, but for the glory to follow at Easter. I pray that my life will always be a celebration of and a tribute to your life and your continued presence with me. Amen.

Song

The song *The Quiet of the Tomb* attempts to imagine Jesus' experience in the tomb. Although there is nothing recorded in Scripture of the time between his burial and his resurrection, it is a significant period for us, as we wait for the resurrection.

Grace found

The Quiet of the Tomb

In the quiet of the tomb, were you waiting,
Anticipating, the coming of day?
Were you still hurting, wounds still aching,
Heart still breaking, from being betrayed?
Only you could know the sacrifice you made,
To carry all my sin with you to the grave.
In the quiet of the tomb, was it stone cold,
A dark and dank hold, where you had to be?
Did you wonder, if I was worthy,
Of all the suffering you bore for me?
Only you could know the sacrifice you made,
To carry all my sin with you to the grave,
In the quiet of the tomb.
Jesus, you would know, not me;
What the weight of my sin would be,
In the quiet of the tomb.
When the angel rolled the stone did you leap out;
Did you dance and shout, there in your glee?
Did you see me, and millions like me,
The ones you set free, eternally?
Only you could make the sacrifice you made,
To hang upon the cross, to die, and then be raised
From the quiet of the tomb.

© 2008 Hildenbrand

Listen to this song at www.ContemplatingGrace.com

Station 14

Jesus is laid in the tomb

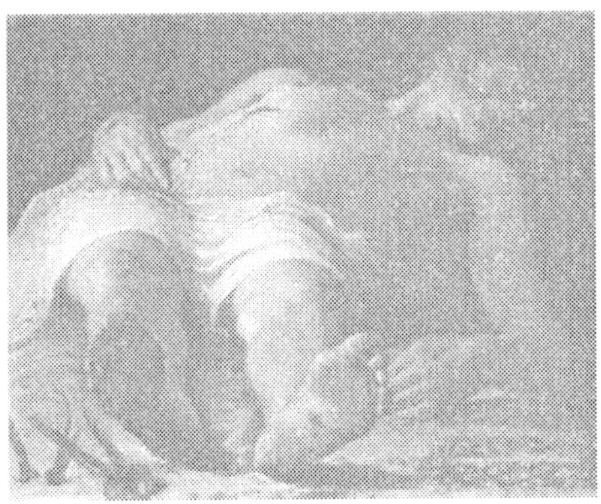

Now there was a good and righteous man named Joseph, who, though a member of the council, had not agreed to their plan and action. He came from the Jewish town of Arimathea, and he was waiting expectantly for the kingdom of God. This man went to Pilate and asked for the body of Jesus. Then he took it down, wrapped it in a linen cloth, and laid it in a rock-hewn tomb where no one had ever been laid. It was the day of Preparation, and the sabbath was beginning.
Luke 23:50-54

Monday after Palm Sunday

Station 14, Day 1: Jesus is laid in the tomb

Now there was a good and righteous man named Joseph, who, though a member of the council, had not agreed to their plan and action. He came from the Jewish town of Arimathea, and he was waiting expectantly for the kingdom of God.
Luke 23:50-51

Meditation

We cannot know how many members of the Sanhedrin opposed Jesus. We do know, however, there were at least two who recognized something that set him apart from other false prophets claiming to be the Messiah – Nicodemus and Joseph of Arimathea. Nicodemus came to Jesus one night to question him alone (John 3:1-21). The author of Luke records that Joseph was "waiting expectantly for the kingdom of God." The fact that he was even present at Jesus' death probably indicates that Joseph recognized Jesus could well be the Messiah. The fact that he remained a member of the Temple leadership probably confirms his uncertainty.

Spiritual discipline

Fast for the next 5 days by altering what you eat for lunch. Perhaps eat only an apple, or at least a significantly smaller quantity of food than normal. When you finish lunch and do not feel satiated, remember Jesus laying in the cold, dark tomb.

Prayer

Understanding Lord, like Nicodemus and Joseph of Arimathea, I often have doubts about you. Too often, I hold to my comfortable traditions and am reluctant to stray from them to reach out to you. Help my unbelief, I pray. Amen.

Grace found

Tuesday after Palm Sunday

Station 14, Day 2: Jesus is laid in the tomb

This man went to Pilate and asked for the body of Jesus. Then he took it down, wrapped it in a linen cloth, and laid it in a rock-hewn tomb where no one had ever been laid. Luke 23:52-53

Meditation

Joseph of Arimathea, one of the Jewish authorities, goes to Pilate for permission to bury the body of Jesus. The lifeless body is removed from the cross, wrapped in cloth, and given to Joseph, who places it in a newly-hewn tomb and leaves it there. A large stone is rolled in front of the entrance to the tomb to secure it.

The fact that no other bodies had been laid in the tomb before is an important detail for fulfilling an Old Testament prophesy.

Spiritual discipline

Meditate for 10 minutes on Jesus in the tomb. Picture yourself standing beside the body. Feel the darkness of the tomb. Is it cold and damp? Absorb the silence. After the chaotic final hours, the body rests. Rest in the presence of Jesus in the tomb.

Prayer

My Jesus, my Savior, traveling the Stations of the Cross with you has left me drained, emotionally and physically. I cannot imagine how it left you feeling. As you now rest and wait, I rest and wait with you. Amen.

Grace found

Wednesday after Palm Sunday

Station 14, Day 3: Jesus is laid in the tomb

It was the day of Preparation, and the sabbath was beginning. Luke 23: 54

Meditation

In the case of Jesus, there was reason for haste in placing his body in a tomb. Jesus died sometime in the afternoon on a Friday, and the Sabbath would begin at sundown. Fridays were days of preparation for the Sabbath. No work was to be done on the Sabbath. Burying a dead body, presumably, was considered work.

It is interesting to me that Jesus' death occurs in time to take his body down from the cross and place it in a tomb before sundown. Even in dying, Jesus honored the traditions of his faith.

Spiritual discipline

Find a quiet place and enter a time of silence for 10 minutes. Attempt to let go of the trials of the moment – your to do list, your stressors at work or home, the pressing needs of family. Deliberately turn off your inner dialogue by acknowledging thoughts as they come to you, then letting them go. Breathe deeply and internalize whatever degree of silence you can attain. There is no pressure to receive insights or inspiration. Experiencing silence is sufficient.

Prayer

Lord Jesus, it is finished. It has been a long, painful journey for you, but now your time on earth is done. Thank you, precious Lord, for taking that journey on my behalf. Amen.

Grace found

Holy Thursday

The Last Supper

And during supper Jesus, knowing that the Father had given all things into his hands, and that he had come from God and was going to God, got up from the table, took off his outer robe, and tied a towel around himself. Then he poured water into a basin and began to wash the disciples' feet and to wipe them with the towel that was tied around him. John 13:2b-5

Then he took a loaf of bread, and when he had given thanks, he broke it and gave it to them, saying, "This is my body, which is given for you. Do this in remembrance of me." And he did the same with the cup after supper, saying, "This cup that is poured out for you is the new covenant in my blood." Luke 22:19-20

Meditation

Although we have completed our study of the Stations of the Cross, tonight the journey begins again. Jesus has a final supper with his closest friends, the 12 disciples. He performs a selfless act of service by washing the feet of the disciples. Because most people walked around barefooted or in sandals, feet were always filthy. Cleaning the feet was the undesirable job of a servant, if the owner of the house had servants. Jesus assumed the role of servant and told the disciples they, too, needed to become servants.

Also at this supper, Jesus initiates the sacrament of communion. He takes bread and wine from the table, blesses it, and shares it with his disciples, telling them to remember him every time they eat and drink. This plea for remembrance was not a narcissistic act. Jesus did not fear being forgotten for self-serving reasons. He feared being forgotten because he knew the disciples, and we today, would need to remember – to remember that Jesus is with us, Jesus is one with God, and through Jesus, we are also one with God.

Spiritual discipline

Attend a Maundy Thursday service at the church of your choice. Hold the picture of Jesus at his last supper in your mind. Meditate for 10 minutes on the events that are about to come. You have walked the Via Dolorosa with Jesus over these past weeks, and you know what is next. Serve as a faithful and patient witness over the next three days.

Prayer

Lord Jesus, wonderful counselor, I will remember you. I will remember this night with you each time I receive communion. I will remember the love you showed through the pain and suffering of your death. Finally, I will remember that you died so I could have life, and have it abundantly. Amen.

Grace found

Good Friday

The Crucifixion

After this, when Jesus knew that all was now finished, he said (in order to fulfill the scripture), "I am thirsty." A jar of sour wine was standing there. So they put a sponge full of the wine on a branch of hyssop and held it to his mouth. When Jesus had received the wine, he said, "It is finished." Then he bowed his head and gave up his spirit. John 19:28-30

When it was noon, darkness came over the whole land until three in the afternoon. At three o'clock Jesus cried out with a loud voice, "Eloi, eloi, lema sabachthani?" which means, "My God, my God, why have your forsaken me?" Then Jesus gave a loud cry and breathed his last. And the curtain of the temple was torn in two, from top to bottom. Mark 15:33-34, 37-38

Meditation

Good Friday appears to be poorly named. What can possibly be "good" about a day that symbolizes the cruel last hours of Jesus? Jesus was first arrested in the Garden of Gethsemane sometime around or after midnight, and the day goes downhill for Jesus after that. Sleepless, beaten, mocked, flogged, bleeding, stumbling under the weight of a heavy cross, Jesus is finally nailed onto the cross and dies. Friends make some haste in getting his body down from the cross and into a tomb before sundown so they do not violate the Sabbath prohibition on work.

It just does not sound like a *good* day for anyone.

Spiritual discipline

Meditate on the images of the events of this day. Review your notes from the last 6 weeks. Take a deep breath and experience the relief as the gruesome journey finally comes to an end. Watch as the body of Jesus is laid to rest in a tomb.

Prayer

Lord Jesus, my prince of peace, as your body lay dead in the tomb, I know there must have been some relief to be finished with the crucifixion. As I review the events of this day, again, I am amazed at your endurance and selfless sacrifice. Give me an uneasy rest this day, knowing this, like all painful parts of our lives, is a necessary part of the glory to come. Amen.

Grace found

Saturday after Palm Sunday (the Sabbath)

On the sabbath they rested according to the commandment. Luke 23:56b

Meditation

Easter is an interesting day of celebration for many reasons, one of which is how the actual day is determined. It is not a specific calendar day, like Christmas or New Year's. It is not a specific day of a specific week, like Thanksgiving. Easter is not determined by human calendars, but by the movements of the created universe. Easter occurs on the first Sunday after the first full moon following the spring equinox. The equinox occurs when the sun is midway on its journey from its high point in the northern sky and its low point in the southern sky.

Scripture is silent on the happenings of the day between the crucifixion and the resurrection. It is the Sabbath – a day of rest. No doubt, for the followers of Jesus who remained faithful to the end, this day of rest was needed to begin recovering from the emotionally draining events of the previous day.

Spiritual Discipline

Fast on this day by refraining from eating any solid food between sunrise and sunset. As your hunger builds during the day, remember the followers of Jesus who, even though they had been told, did not know Jesus would be resurrected tomorrow morning. Meditate on the lost and hopeless feeling they experienced. Experience the despair with them.

Prayer

Crucified Lord, on this day of rest, on this day of recuperation, I make my final preparations for your resurrection. A part of me has died with you on this journey. I pray you will resurrect a new me with you tomorrow, a me that is a more faithful and devoted follower of you in all my ways and for all my days on earth. Amen.

Grace found

Easter Sunday

But on the first day of the week, at early dawn, they came to the tomb, taking the spices that they had prepared. They found the stone rolled away from the tomb, but when they went in, they did not find the body. While they were perplexed about this, suddenly two men in dazzling clothes stood beside them. The women were terrified and bowed their faces to the ground, but the men said to them, "Why do you look for the living among the dead? He is not here, but has risen."
Luke 24:1-5

Meditation

Why look for the living among the dead? Mary Magdalene and others went to the tomb looking for Jesus, but he was no longer there. Tombs are for the dead, but Jesus had been resurrected and was alive. He appeared many times in the subsequent days to the disciples and others, providing final counsel prior to ascending into heaven.

In order to experience the renewal of resurrection, we must first go through crucifixion – a part of us must die. Sometimes those types of deaths are extremely painful. Once we have been through that death, however, we must allow the dead part of us to pass. We cannot begin a new and resurrected life until we let go of the old one.

Why do we look for the living among the dead? Whenever we attempt to hold onto the way things used to be, we seek the living among the dead. When our thoughts and feelings focus on things of the past, we cannot be fully present to the now. We must learn to let go of the past because the living are not there.

Spiritual discipline

Attend an Easter service at the church of your choice. Experience the joy of the resurrection of Jesus, as well as what it represents in you.

Prayer

Resurrected Christ, Lord of my life, the joy of this day is inexpressible. Because of the nature of your death, I know there is nothing I can suffer that you will not understand. Because of your resurrection, I can know the joy of rebirth! Remind me to stay in the present with the living. Thank you for your wonderful grace and the promise that you will never leave me. In your most holy name I pray, Amen.

Grace found

Greg Hildenbrand

He's Alive!

Mary was the first to find the open, empty tomb,
At first light on the third day past his crucifixion swoon;
Angels sat inside the tomb where once his body laid,
And said, "Our Lord's been risen from the grave!"
"Oh sister, tell me why you seek the living with the dead?
He is not here, he's risen, just the way that he had said,
Now go to his disciples and proclaim it far and wide:
'He is not dead! He's risen! He's alive!'"
But he had died, was crucified, they nailed him to a tree,
That he'd return to life again was too much to believe;
Until we saw the stone removed and the empty tomb inside,
The angels sang the glad refrain, "Our Lord's been glorified!
He's alive! He's alive!"
"Peace be with you all as to my God I now ascend,
Blest are you who saw me die and watched me rise again!
More blessed still are those who have not seen and yet believe,
My peace I give to all who will receive!"
But he had died, was crucified, they nailed him to a tree,
That he'd return to life again was too much to believe;
Until we saw the stone removed and the empty tomb inside,
The angels sang the glad refrain, "Our Lord's been glorified!
He's alive! He's alive! He's alive! He's alive!

© 2002 Hildenbrand

Listen to this song at www. ContemplatingGrace.Com

Postscript

In *Finding Grace in Lent,* I attempt to provide a focused study for the period from Ash Wednesday to Easter, using the Stations of the Cross as a template. On the one hand, the journey is excruciatingly detailed and deliberate. On the other hand, there are lessons of significance I skipped or skimmed over in my narrative to preserve the book's format. Without a doubt, there are additional insights I have yet to discover.

In the spirit of blessings-yet-to-be-uncovered, I believe an on-going reflection on the journey to the cross is worthwhile for contemplative Christians. Although I am not a Catholic, I admire the place of honor given to the *Stations of the Cross* in many Catholic churches. The Stations are visible as one enters and are present and accessible year-round for meditation, prayer, and reflection.

I encourage the reader to keep this book handy and review its contents throughout the year. Likewise, I encourage the regular use of meditation, fasting, and silence as on-going practices. The lessons of the crucifixion and resurrection are timeless and grace-filled. Although the story is not always pleasant or entertaining, the same can be said about our lives. Jesus' final hours hold a vital lesson for us, however. There is purpose in our suffering, and God will make good things grow out of our most difficult trials.

May you experience God's amazing grace, now and always!

Greg Hildenbrand
January 2015

Endnotes

All scripture references are from the *New Interpreter's Study Bible, New Revised Standard Version with the Apocrypha*, by the Abingdon Press, Nashville. 2003.

Acknowledgements

I offer my appreciation to the Reverend Stan Hughes, a walking partner and contemplative brother in the faith, for reviewing and providing insightful feedback on the contents of this book.

My daughter, Grace, assisted with the review and editing of these pages. She, of course, was a blessing to me long before she acquired her considerable skills in communication.

My friend and fellow musician, Billy Pilgrim (BillyPilgrim.biz), applied his amazing design talents to the book cover.

My friend and fellow musician, Ron Vaughn (RonVaugh.net), added percussive sweetening to most of the songs that are referenced in these pages.

My son, Reid, is one of the most earnest seekers of God's truth I know. He is an on-going source of inspiration for me.

My wife, Carrie, has been a constant source of strength and encouragement since our marriage in 1987.

Any shortcomings in this work are in spite of – not because of – the efforts of these talented professionals and loving family members. For their unique and vital contributions I am humbled and sincerely thankful.

About the Author

Greg Hildenbrand is a leader of contemporary and blended worship at the First United Methodist Church in Lawrence, Kansas. He has written and recorded dozens of songs, many of which are a regular part of worship. He is the author of the book *Finding Grace in an Imperfect World*, as well as of *Life Notes,* a weekly meditation which contemplates the presence of God in our everyday lives. A collection of Greg's writings is available at www.ContemplatingGrace.Com.

Greg is also the Executive Director for *Life Star of Kansas,* a not-for-profit provider of critical care transport services in northeast Kansas. Greg and his wife, Carrie, live near Lawrence, Kansas, and have two adult children, Grace and Reid.

Communicate with Greg at ghildenbrand@sunflower.com, or through his website, www.ContemplatingGrace.Com.